Scarborough *Past*

SCARBOROUGH
Evening News

at heart publications

First Published in 2007 by:
At Heart Ltd, 32 Stamford Street, Altrincham,
Cheshire, WA14 1EY.

in conjunction with

The Scarborough Evening News,
17-23 Aberdeen Walk, Scarborough,
North Yorkshire YO11 1BB

Printed by Bell & Bain, Scotland.

ISBN: 978-1-84547-166-8

Foreword

THIS *Scarborough Evening News* publication reflects the affection for Britain's first holiday resort.

Recent endeavours have created significant new environmental, cultural, tourism and leisure developments which herald a new era for the Queen of Resorts.

The new horizon is an ideal opportunity to reflect on Scarborough over the past century.

The following images of some of its most recognisable locations remind us of a time that kept hat-makers in business – and when life seemed to roll along with more tranquillity. The scenery and streets (free from yellow parking lines and multiple directional signs), the fashions and the fun comprise files of social history, as well as create nostalgia.

The derivations of the name 'Scarborough' are lost in time.

One suggestion refers to the town's geographical features because the old Norse word 'sker' means a high, open area on a hill face, or a cliff or promontory. Hence the name of a headland and its settlement.

But the piratical Viking Thorgils, who set sail to the sounds of horns from Iceland to roam around Britain and Ireland and who directed his crew to the Yorkshire coast in 966AD, is also credited with the derivation. His nickname was Skarthi, meaning harelip. On the basis of this connection, Scarborough is named by the combination of a fortress (burg) and a marauder with a facial deformity.

Bronze Age settlers, Roman soldiers, Saxons and Normans preceded the influx of friendlier 'invaders' who arrived for the Spa waters or sea-bathing in the 17th century.

Much later, many people were attracted by the delights of Peasholm Park and lake, the old North Bay attractions such as the Open-Air Theatre and The Corner with its waffles, or by the beach pierrots, seaside theatres or the Aquarium Top and Gala Land. Others came then, as now, simply for the pleasure of the foreshore or to admire the remarkable view of the Old Town and harbour from the Esplanade.

Scarborough's railway era began in the 1840s and massively added to the resort's growth. A century later, Scarborough's image was further boosted by a series of stylish railway posters.

Throughout the changes, there has been one feature of universal, perennial attraction – the perfect, gently-sloping sandy arcs of South Bay and North Bay beaches.

Our Scarborough has spawned 16 others across the globe, a few of them with similar bays.

The seascape, and all life under the vigilance of the castle keep and its headland, have been recorded by the *Evening News* since July 10 1882.

The newspaper was established by the Whittaker family and was, at one time, just one of seven newspapers, including two dailies, in the town. Its sister newspapers under Johnston Press now include titles for Whitby, Bridlington, Filey, Malton, Pickering, Driffield, Pocklington and Beverley – and the *Yorkshire Post*, to which we are grateful for its invaluable contribution to this archive.

The *Evening News* is now a multi-media company, with SEN TV video news footage on www.scarborough'eveningnews.co.uk but the power of print is still with us and I hope the simplicity and variety of this volume bring you immense joy, and revive many happy memories.

Ed Asquith
Editor, *Scarborough Evening News*

The southern end of Foreshore Road – complete with a "Dr Who"-style police phone-box at the entrance to the Aquarium Top, which is out of shot on the left. The picture was taken on August 29, 1959. Image: SP001

The busy crossroads at the junction of the Aquarium Top, Lower Ramshill Road (on the left), Valley Road and Vernon Road (on the right), pictured around the end of the 1950s. Image: SP002

Pictured from the Aquarium Top in July 1964 are the Rotunda Museum, with part of the roof of the subterranean Gala Land entertainments complex in front of it, and, on the right, part of the imposing Grand Hotel. Image: SP003

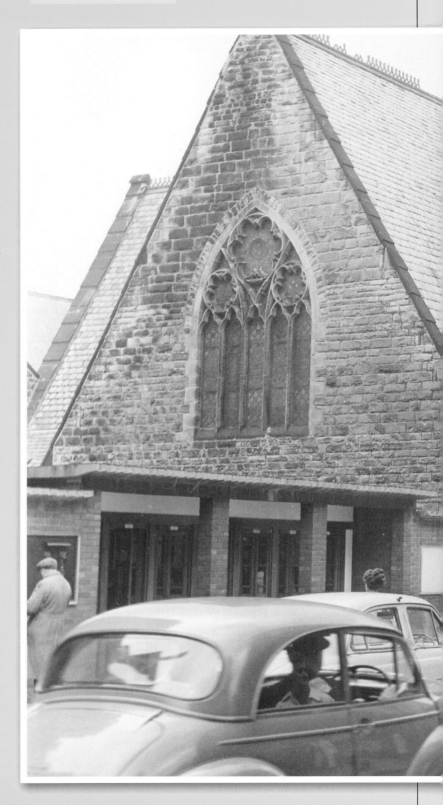

■ The Aberdeen Walk side of Bar Congregational Church, at the junction with Westborough, in 1963. Image: SP004

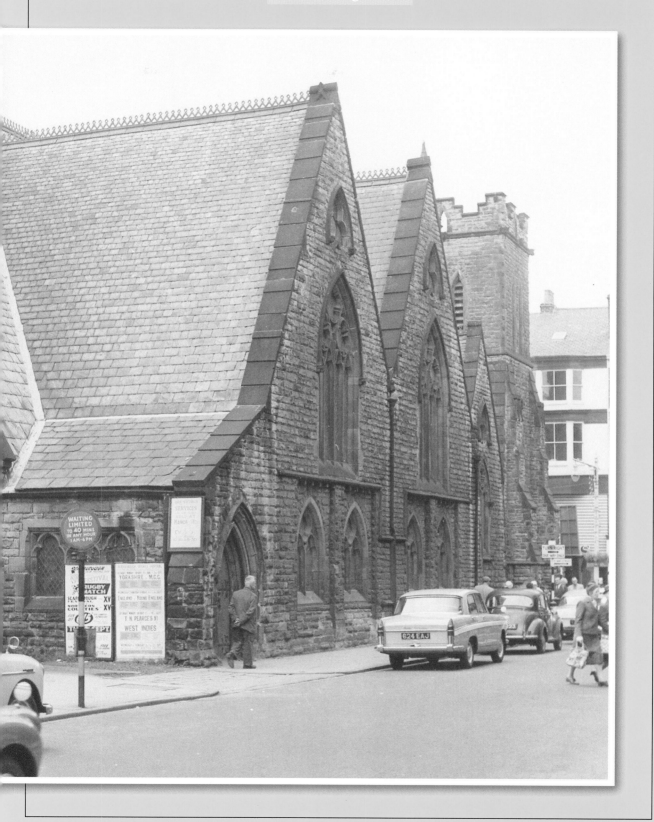

Part of Bar Congregational Church, which stood at the corner of Aberdeen Walk and Westborough. This view was taken from the Aberdeen Walk side in 1963. Image: SP005

Westborough in 1963, with Bar Congregational Church prominent at the Aberdeen Walk junction. James Beal's men's and boys' outfitters, on the other Aberdeen Walk corner, was one of the best-known shops in Scarborough for many years. Image: SP006

The herring season at Scarborough in the early 1900s. Holidaymakers pictured to the left of the Lighthouse Pier are watching the Scottish fisher lassies who followed their fishermen menfolk down the East Coast, gutting the herring and packing them in salt in barrels to preserve them. Scarborough herring was exported all over Northern Europe.

The steam drifter in the foreground, the *Lustre Gem*, was registered at Banff. It was in port when the photograph was taken because herring fishing was done at night. Image: SP007

The Aquarium Top area in the early 1960s, showing the Spa Bridge, with the roof of the Gala Land subterranean entertainments complex below and to the left of it. Image: SP008

The Pavilion Hotel, which stood for a century at what was Scarborough's busiest crossroads until modern traffic changes. The hotel was owned for many years by the Laughton family – one of whom was the famous Hollywood actor Charles. The crossroads, near the railway station, is where Westborough, Northway and Valley Bridge Road meet. Image: SP009

Two very popular places of entertainment on Foreshore Road – both now long since demolished. On the right is the Olympia and on the left what was known as the Windmill building, from the big illuminated wooden motif on the front. The Windmill was then being used as an amusement arcade. Between the two buildings is the bottom station of a cliff tramway, advertising fares at only 3p. Image: SP010

■ The originally elegant Pavilion Square, off Valley Bridge Road and behind the Pavilion Hotel. Part of the square was used as a car park for the hotel, and at one period there were tennis courts there. The square went sadly downhill later, but following threat of demolition it was saved. Image: SP0011

The picture was taken during a big redevelopment project at the corner of Queen Street and Newborough, which opened up this view of the Market Street side of Boyes department store for a short period. Image: SP012

In the middle of the picture is the popular Peasholm Park, with its lake, floating bandstand, and, to the right, its island topped by a pagoda. In the foreground are the Alexandra Gardens bowling greens. Image: SP013

The construction of the Marine Drive, which took from 1897 until 1908. Steam cranes can be seen at work in the far distance, near a surviving prominent feature of the coastline called the Coffee Pot Rock. The area in the foreground where construction materials are being stored was at the eastern end of the Royal Albert Drive, which was completed in 1890, and which the Marine Drive was to extend round the foot of Castle Hill. Image: SP014

The tides governed a lot of the work of building the Marine Drive – as in the case of this construction at the foot of the sea wall which was covered by the sea except for brief periods either side of low tide twice a day. Image: SP015a/015b

The white marks on the roof of this prominent building in Ramshill Road point to a previous and more-upmarket use. They are the remains of the word "BATHS" – from the time a century and more ago when the building was aimed at people who came to Scarborough for their health, in a period when medicinal and saltwater bathing were popular cure-alls. Image: SP016

County Garages, which stood in St Thomas Street, was for many years the Scarborough town terminus of buses serving country areas. Image: SP017

The Scalby Mills tourist development built in the mid-1960s. By that time a lot of British holiday-makers were going abroad for guaranteed sunshine, and the development was not a success. A popular sea life centre now stands on the site. Image: SP018

The Scalby Mills Hotel was a popular pub for holidaymakers at the Scalby Mills visitor complex. Just to the left of the hotel is one of the locomotives of the North Bay Miniature Railway. Image: SP019

Vernon Road, with, on the left, part of a borough council surface car park on which a Woolworth's store extension and part of the Brunswick Centre shopping complex were later built. The church tower seen above the building in the middle of the picture belonged to the now-demolished Christ Church. Image: SP020

■ Part of Vernon Road, with, in the background, Scarborough Central Library, and above it the tower of Christ Church. Image: SP021

■ St Thomas Street. On the left, just beyond Burkin's shoe repairers, is the Royal Opera House – which has now been replaced by a casino. Image: SP022

The big Rowntree's – and later Debenham's – department store dominated a very big site bounded by Westborough and York Place. Image: SP023

St Thomas Street and its junction with Newborough, seen from St Nicholas Street. The prominent building on the right housed a Coopland's baker's and grocer's shop on the ground floor and a cafe above. Image: SP024

Part of Westborough, as seen from Aberdeen Walk on a wet day in the early 1960s, with the John Smith's pub the County Hotel prominent in the middle of the picture. It later became a dress shop. Image: SP025

The corner of Victoria Road and Northway. The block of buildings nearest the camera in Victoria Road, between Northway and Barwick Street, was demolished to make way for a new Scarborough police station, which was opened in 1965. Image: SP026

■ This aerial photograph taken in August 1952 shows how far the Castle Hill headland thrusts out into the North Sea.
Image: SP027

The North Bay Bathing Pool, as it was then called, seen in aerial photographs taken in May 1947. It later had several other names. The ribbon of water on the left of the top picture is part of Peasholm Park lake, fringing the park's island. Image: SP028

Low tide in the South Bay in August 1954. The outer harbour is almost completely dry and there is only a dribble of water in the entrance to the inner harbour and alongside the fish market on the West Pier. Image: SP029

Alongside the middle pier in this August 1952 aerial shot of the harbour is a three-masted tall ship called the *Hispaniola* – having been used as the vessel of that name during the shooting of a 1950 film of *Treasure Island*. When the photograph was taken the ship was being used by Scarborough Council to house an aquarium display. Image: SP030

The North Bay Bathing Pool, as it was then called, had been opened less than a month when this aerial photograph of it taken on August 2, 1938. The pool later had several other names. Beyond the pool, towards the sea, is the Corner Café. In the top left of the picture are some of the many tennis courts that were then on the high ground between the Open Air Theatre and the North Bay cliff. The ribbon of water at the bottom of the picture is part of Peasholm Park lake.
Image: SP031

Front and centre of this aerial picture taken in August 1952 is the West Pier, with its fish market, baiting-shed buildings, and, at the landward end, the Lifeboathouse. Image: SP032

The central part of the North Side pictured from the air in August 1952. Facilities to be seen, from the left, are the Alexandra Gardens bowling greens, the North Bay cliff tramway, Peasholm Park with its lake and island, the Corner Cafe, and the North Bay Bathing Pool. The small boats at the water's edge tell how popular the North Bay was with holidaymakers then. The boats belonged to fishermen who thought it worth while to sail round from the South Bay to get passengers for short pleasure trips. Image: SP033

There were relatively few boats in Scarborough Harbour when this aerial shot was taken in June 1946. Things were still getting back to normal then following the Second World War. Image: SP034

■ The prominent Grand Hotel casts a vast shadow across the South Bay beach in this aerial picture taken in August 1954. Image: SP035

■ There were quite a number of fishing boats moored by the fish-market buildings on the West Pier when this aerial picture was taken in May 1959. As always the beach is filled with locals and holidaymakers in sunny weather. Image: SP036

■ The main attractions of the North
Bay in May 1947 seen from the air
include the Corner Cafe, the North
Bay Bathing Pool, Peasholm Park,
and, on the left, one of the
Alexandra Gardens bowling greens.
Image: SP037

■ This sweep of the South Bay
from the harbour round to beyond
the Spa was captured from the air
in July 1949. Image: SP038

There was plenty of room on the south sands when this aerial picture was taken in August 1954, it being just about extreme low tide.

Image: SP039

The relatively few people on the south beach on a fine summer's day was most probably due to the fact that when the picture was taken in July 1945 the Second World War had only just ended and many men and women were still away from home, serving in the armed forces. Image: SP040

A short wooden jetty for small pleasure craft – irreverently called the Chicken Run by generations of harbour users – had been constructed in the outer harbour when this picture was taken from the air in August 1957. Image: SP041

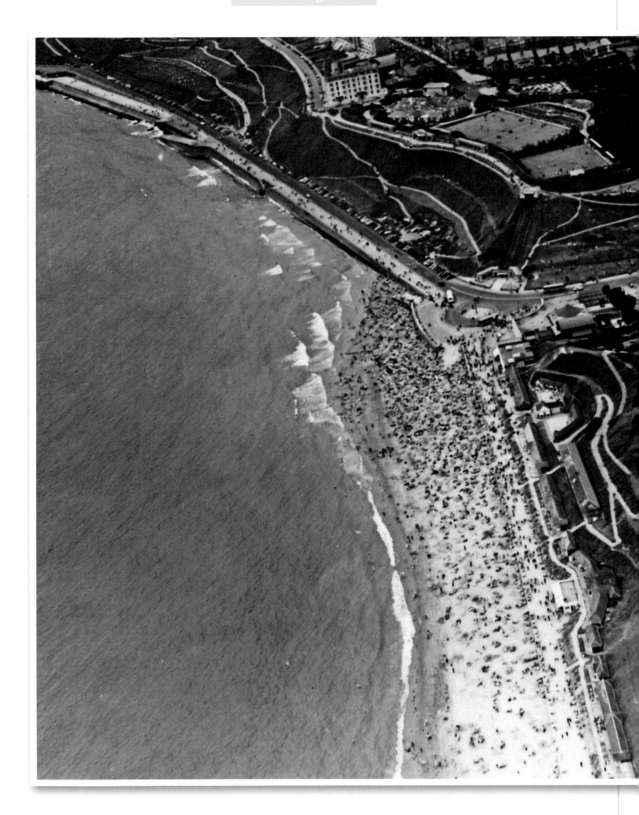

This aerial view taken in May 1959 shows well the mass of red tiled roofs of houses in part of the Old Town behind Foreshore Road at the bottom right. Image: SP042

Leisure facilities of the North Bay pictured from the air in August 1957 include the Corner Café, the North Bay Bathing Pool, Peasholm Park, Alexandra Gardens bowling greens at the top, and some of the tennis courts above Northstead Manor Gardens at the lower right. While the roads appear to be fairly empty, the same cannot be said about the beach. Image: SP043

The boats seen in the South Bay were no doubt waiting for the tide to rise enough to allow them to get into at least the bottom end of the harbour. The aerial photograph was taken in August 1954. Image: SP044

Leisure facilities of the North Bay pictured from the air in August 1957 include the Corner Café, the North Bay Bathing Pool, Peasholm Park, and Alexandra Gardens bowling greens at the left. Image: SP045

The big light-coloured boat in the bottom right-hand corner of the harbour in this 1950s aerial picture was a floating HQ for Sea Cadets. Image: SP046

Homes and other building in Scarborough's Old Town nestling between the harbour and the Castle Hill, which gives shelter from cold northerly winds in winter. The photograph was taken in August 1957. Image: SP047

The almost complete absence of cars on the Marine Drive – one of the busiest parking spots in Scarborough during the holiday season – is explained by the fact the picture was taken in May 1947, when petrol was still rationed and there were still relatively very few private cars on the roads.

Image: SP048

This hole beside the road on the Aquarium Top was what remained after the demolition of what for many years was Scarborough's only public indoor swimming pool. It was originally built as part of the subterranean Aquarium complex, and generations of schoolchildren were taken there for swimming lessons. It never reopened after the Second World War, when it was used by the RAF for survival exercises by aircrew trainees. Image: SP049

■ A rare very early aerial picture of Scarborough. Taken on August 2, 1938, it shows the sweep of the North Bay over the castle headland, with Jackson's Bay beyond it. mage: SP050

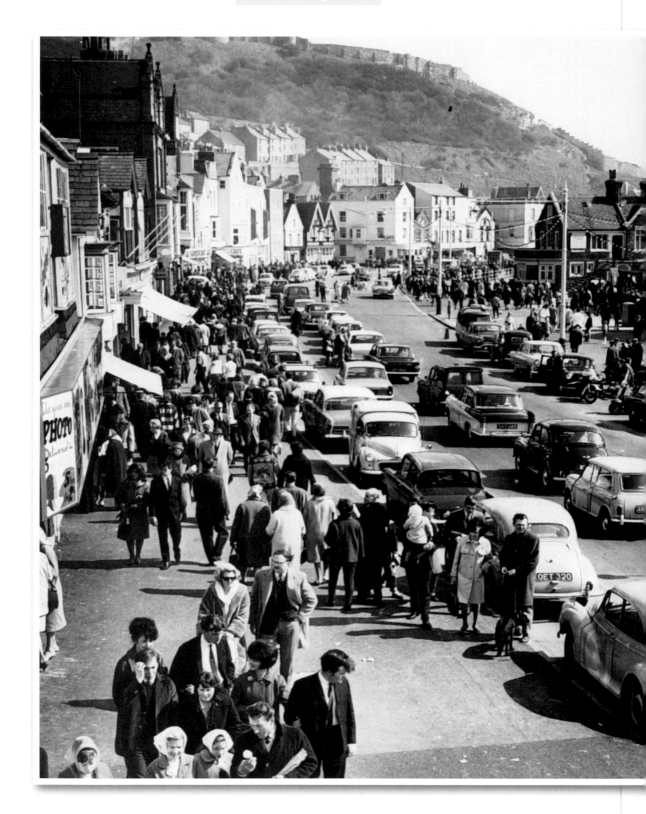

This view of Scarborough Castle's keep and defensive walls shows why attackers over the years found it such a tough nut to crack. The picture was taken in March 1974. Image: SP051

Looking along the South Bay seafront from Foreshore Road to Sandside in April 1965, the pavements are teeming with holidaymakers. The large buildings on the right are at the shore end of the West Pier, and the one nearer the camera is the Lifeboathouse. Image: SP052

The so-called King Richard III House on Sandside. The king is reputed to have stayed there during one of his visits to Scarborough in the late 1400s, when he was engaged in making the town his main naval base for operations against his Scottish enemies. The house was opened to the public as a privately owned museum for many years. When this picture was taken in May 1964 the next-door antiques shop was in the same ownership. Image: SP053

Scarborough's ancient parish church, St Mary's, near the castle. The grave of novelist Anne Brontë, who died in Scarborough in 1849, is in St Mary's churchyard beside Castle Road. Image: SP054

One of the many quaint old streets in the Old Town – this one photographed in June 1949. Image: SP055

The view down Newborough, from near its junctions with St Thomas Street and St Nicholas Street, in August 1947. Image: SP056

■ Oliver's Mount on the left dominates this September 1959 view across the outer harbour, the South Bay, and the Spa. The high column of a memorial to Scarborough's dead of the two World Wars on top of Oliver's Mount can be seen from much of the town. Image: SP057

The junction of Westborough and Northway in November 1960. On the left is what was then the Odeon Cinema – now the Stephen Joseph Memorial Theatre. On the other side of Northway is part of what was then a new block of shops with flats above which has drawn much criticism as being unworthy of the prominent site. Image: SP058

In the bottom left of this 1960s aerial photograph is Scarborough Cricket Club's North Marine Road ground – the home of its famed annual Cricket Festival. Beyond the cricket ground are North Side visitor attractions and residential areas. Image: SP059

The bigger of two children's model-boat ponds in Peasholm Glen pictured in April 1968. Image: SP060

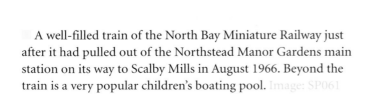

A well-filled train of the North Bay Miniature Railway just after it had pulled out of the Northstead Manor Gardens main station on its way to Scalby Mills in August 1966. Beyond the train is a very popular children's boating pool. Image: SP061

Scarborough Town Hall – originally a wealthy banker's 19th century home – photographed in March 1945, when the Second World War was still being fought in Europe and in the Far East. Image: SP062

A covering of snow gives a striking and unusual look to this sweep of the North Bay, as seen from a point a little to the south of Peasholm Gap and the Corner Café. Image: SP063

The view was from the top of Oliver's Mount in July 1949. There have been many changes in the intervening decades. Image: SP064

King Richard III House on Sandside, where the monarch is said to have stayed in the late 1400s during a visit when he was making Scarborough his main naval base in the north of England. The privately owned building was for many years a show-house and small museum. Image: SP065

The Oliver's Mount racing circuit is mainly known as a top track for motorcycling events. But it has been a venue for car races since it was established in 1946 – as this 1955 picture shows. Image: SP066

Cars running the gauntlet of towering waves breaking against the Marine Drive in 1958. Many cars attempting to go round the Drive in stormy weather have, over the years, been stopped in their tracks with their ignition systems swamped. Some people have had to be rescued from their cars by the emergency services, and at least one vehicle and its occupants were saved from being washed into the sea only by the iron railings on the edge of the Drive's footpath. Image: SP067

Sidecar outfits going round the Memorial Hairpin during a motorcycle race meeting on the Oliver's Mount racing circuit in July 1955. The corner gets its name from the town's memorial to its dead of the two World Wars, seen on the left. Image: SP068

The start of a solo motorbike race on the Oliver's Mount circuit in July 1955, with a big crowd of spectators on the natural grandstand area to the right of the picture. Image: SP069

Solo riders rounding the Mere Hairpin on the Oliver's Mount motorcycle racing circuit in July 1955 before heading up a stiff climb to the highest part of the track. Image: SP070

The builders of Scarborough Castle exploited the natural topography brilliantly. The pictured narrow point between the heavily fortified barbican defending the main gate to the left and the ascent to the main part of the castle and its keep to the right must have been easy to defend. And especially when there was a drawbridge there instead of the fixed bridge in the 1956 picture. In the background is the North Bay. Image: SP071

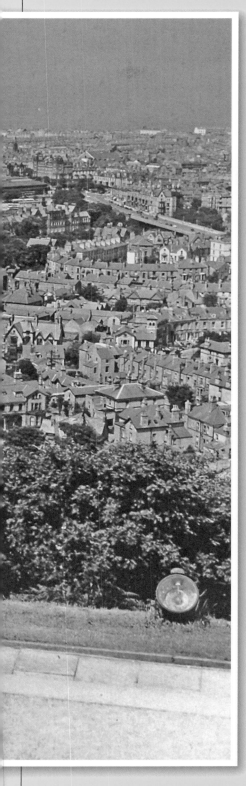

The North Bay Miniature Railway received wide publicity in June 1955 because its trains were among the few still running in the country as a strike hit British Rail services. Image: SP072

This view was taken from the top of Oliver's Mount in July 1959. The town's built-up area has expanded markedly, with much new housing. Image: SP073

A North Bay Miniature Railway train gets a send-off from a crowd on a bridge above it in Northstead Manor Gardens in May 1945. World War Two had not ended at that time but lots of people were obviously in holiday mood after nearly six years of conflict. Image: SP074

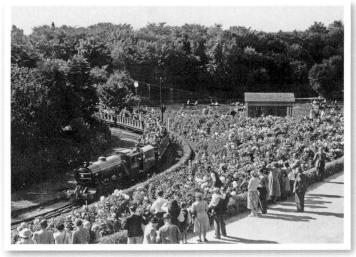

A North Bay Miniature Railway train just about to pull into the main station in Northstead Manor Gardens in August 1949. Image: SP075

The colourful Italian Gardens below the South Cliff's Esplanade – one of Scarborough's most tranquil spots. The picture dates from May 1957. Image: SP076

An easterly storm in 1958 closes the Royal Albert Drive to all but the very brave and the foolhardy – and they provide some excitement for the crowd of onlookers in the bottom of the picture, standing in front of the Corner Café. Image: SP077

The half-destroyed 12th century keep of Scarborough Castle shrouded in scaffolding and undergoing maintenance in November 1947. Part of the keep collapsed after bombardment of the Royalist-held castle by Parliamentarian besiegers in 1645 during the Civil War.   Image: SP078

Peasholm Park in February 1947, with a number of skaters on the frozen lake. The winter of 1946-47 was Scarborough's coldest in living memory, and the ice on the lake was thick enough to bear the weight of up to hundreds of people for some six weeks or so. Image: SP079

The winter of 1946 was also cold, but not as bitter as that of 1947. This picture was taken in Peasholm Park in February 1946. Image: SP080

The *Yorkshire Lady*, which took thousands upon thousands of holidaymakers on trips along the coast, in the inner harbour in June 1957. Image: SP081

Song of Norway was the musical given by Scarborough Amateur Operatic Society at the Open Air Theatre in the summer of 1951. Image: SP082

A scene from *King's Rhapsody*, the summer musical show presented at the Open Air Theatre in 1956. Image: SP083

■ This picture was undoubtedly taken in 1951 to record a them-and-us situation on the Spa Bridge which was just about to come to an end.

The bridge was built to be the main approach to the Spa by the private company that then ran it, and it had Spa pay-boxes at the St Nicholas Cliff end.

The railing running along the middle of the bridge was to segregate those who had bought tickets for the Spa (using the wider section on the right) from those paying only a small toll to use the bridge merely as a short cut between St Nicholas Cliff and the South Cliff. The bridge was for years known as The Halfpenny Bridge after the first toll charge.

The picture was taken on July 12, 1951. A week later the bridge was freed of toll by the borough council, which had bought it from the Spa Company, and the Spa pay-boxes were closed and their turnstiles removed. The middle railing was taken down some time later. Image: SP084

The South Bay and castle headland pictured from a cliff pathway above the Spa in September 1963. Image: SP085

This aerial picture was taken on a sunny day in early August. The lack of vehicles on the Marine Drive is down to the fact that the year was 1938, when the majority of holiday visitors to Scarborough travelled by train. Image: SP086

The majestic sweep of the North Bay, captured from the North Cliff near the top of Chain Hill.

Image: SP087

Naval vessel *HMS Hesperus* in Scarborough's South Bay during a visit to the town in June 1946.
Image: SP088

By July 1947 most men and women called up for service during the Second World War were back in civilian life and holiday towns were booming – though, as this shot in the North Bay near the Corner Café shows, road traffic was still distinctly light. Image: SP089

Much of older Scarborough is built on land which rises quite markedly from the South Bay seafront. This picture was taken in May 1947. Image: SP090

The most popular part of the south beach in August 1954. Image: SP091

The South Bay captured from the air in June 1946. Image: SP092

■ The tide must have been ebbing when this picture was taken in June 1960, judging by how much of the beach is still damp enough to deter holidaymakers. Image: SP093

The south end of the Marine Drive, with its one-time tollhouse, and the amusements on a wooden decking built over part of the outer harbour, pictured in June 1960. Image: SP094

Main routes into Scarborough from the west show up well in this April 1953 aerial photograph. Image: SP095

This building, at the south end of the Marine Drive, was originally the main place for collecting tolls to use the roadway round the castle headland. There was also a North Tollhouse for many years, but it was in a very exposed position and was demolished after getting into a poor state. The last tolls were lifted in December 1950. This picture dates from August 1961. Image: SP096

The long sweep of the South Bay from the castle headland round to the South Bay Bathing Pool in August 1938. Image: SP097

Four lads – probably locals, since the picture was taken in February 1951 – on the slipway in the inner harbour between the West Pier and the North Wharf. Image: SP098

Three trawlers moored alongside the West Pier's fish market in August 1947. Image: SP099

Scarborough Harbour at dusk, photographed in 1967. Image: SP100

Reflections in the wet south sands of the Grand Hotel and holidaymakers in September 1960. Image: SP101

The Castle Hill looking even more dramatic than usual, thanks to a fresh covering of snow. The picture was taken in February 1946 from a point on the top of the North Cliff near the Alexandra Gardens. Image: SP102